science
technology

HOW THINGS WORK

A Cherrytree Book

Designed and produced by
A S Publishing

First published 1988
by Cherrytree Press Ltd
a subsidiary of
The Chivers Company Ltd
Windsor Bridge Road
Bath, Avon BA2 3AX

Copyright © Cherrytree Press Ltd 1988

British Library Cataloguing in Publication Data
Kerrod, Robin
  How things work.
  1. Science.   Experiments – For children
  I. Title   II. Atkinson, Michael
  III. Atkinson, Sarah
  507'.24

  ISBN 0-7451-5021-7

Printed in Italy by New Interlitho, Milan

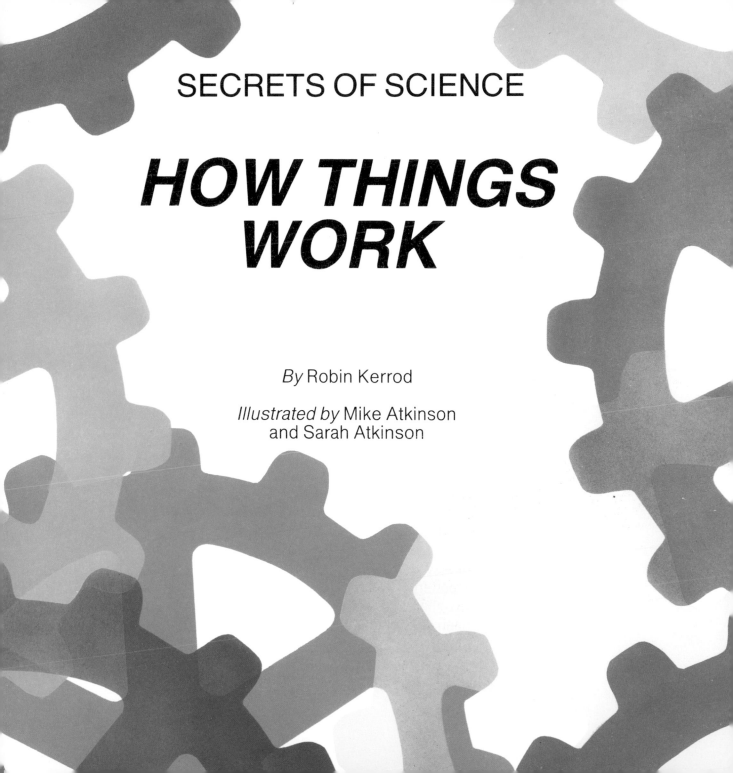

SECRETS OF SCIENCE

HOW THINGS WORK

By Robin Kerrod

Illustrated by Mike Atkinson
and Sarah Atkinson

Safety First

☐ Ask your parents or another adult before you start any experiment, especially if you are using matches or anything hot, sharp or poisonous.

☐ Don't wear your best clothes. Wear old ones or an overall.

☐ If you work on a table, use an old one and protect it with paper or cardboard.

☐ Do water experiments in the sink, on the draining board or outside.

☐ Strike matches away from your body and make sure they are out before you throw them away.

☐ Make sure candles are standing securely.

☐ Wear oven gloves when handling anything hot.

☐ Take care when cutting things. Always cut away from your body.

☐ Don't use tins with jagged edges. Use ones with lids.

☐ Use only safe, non-sniffable children's glue, glue sticks or paste.

☐ Never taste chemicals, unless the book tells you to.

☐ Label all bottles and jars containing chemicals, and store them where young children can't get at them – and not in the family food cupboard.

☐ Never use or play with mains electricity. It can KILL. Use a torch or lantern battery.

☐ When you have finished an experiment, put your things away, clean up and wash your hands.

Contents

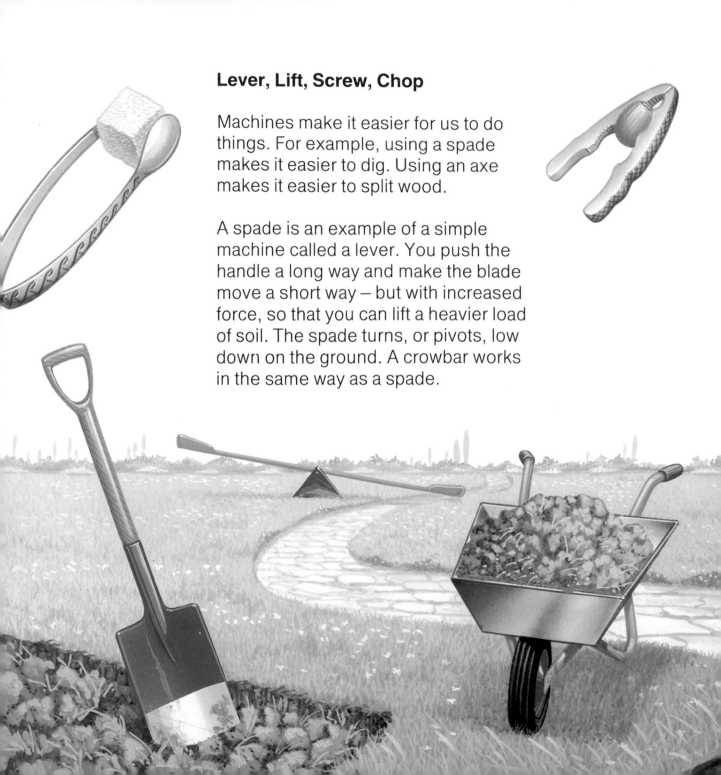

Lever, Lift, Screw, Chop

Machines make it easier for us to do things. For example, using a spade makes it easier to dig. Using an axe makes it easier to split wood.

A spade is an example of a simple machine called a lever. You push the handle a long way and make the blade move a short way — but with increased force, so that you can lift a heavier load of soil. The spade turns, or pivots, low down on the ground. A crowbar works in the same way as a spade.

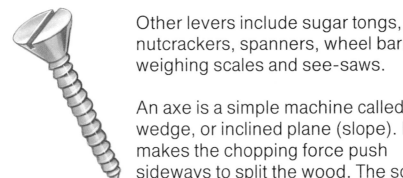

Other levers include sugar tongs, nutcrackers, spanners, wheel barrows, weighing scales and see-saws.

An axe is a simple machine called a wedge, or inclined plane (slope). It makes the chopping force push sideways to split the wood. The screw and the helter-skelter are examples of a continuous inclined plane. The helter-skelter idea is used in mountain roads. Going up a gently sloping road is much easier than going up a steep one.

Wheels at Work

The most important simple machine of all is the wheel. When things move, they rub against each other. This rubbing is called friction, and it slows things down. Wheels make things move more easily because they reduce friction.

Try pushing a heavy load, such as a pile of bricks, along the ground. It's difficult, isn't it? Put the bricks on top of a row of pencils, and see how easily they move. The pencils roll like little wheels, and lower the friction with the ground.

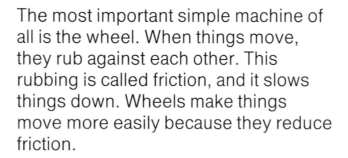

Gears are wheels with teeth around the outside. The teeth of two gears lock together so that one turns the other. When they are different sizes, they turn at different speeds. There are lots of little gear wheels inside ordinary clocks and watches. They drive the hour and minute hands at different speeds.

A Reel Roller

1 You need a cotton reel, an elastic band, two matchsticks and some sticky tape.

2 Thread the elastic band through the hole in the reel and anchor it at one end with a matchstick and tape.

3 Put another matchstick through the band at the other end and wind it round and round.

4 Place the reel on the ground, let go and watch it roll.

Reely Helpful

A pulley makes it easier to lift heavy loads. It has one or more wheels with ropes passing over them. You can make a pulley using cotton reels.

Make a Pulley

1 You need two cotton reels, four screw hooks, some stiff but bendable wire, some string, a heavy load such as a toy bucket full of sand, a wooden bar or shelf to hang your pulleys from, and permission to use it!

2 Screw four hooks into the wood.

3 Tie a loop of wire through a cotton reel, knot it firmly and hang it from the first hook. This is a pulley.

4 Tie one end of a piece of string to your load and put the other over the cotton reel. Pull on the string and see how easily it lifts.

5 Now make another pulley and this time attach it to the load.

6 Attach one end of a piece of string to your second hook, loop it through the pulley, and pull. Is it easier to lift the load?

7 Take both of the pulleys you have made and use them together. Tie your string to the fourth hook, then loop it first through the pulley attached to the load, and then through a pulley attached to the third hook.

8 Now pull on the string and see how much lighter your load seems this time.

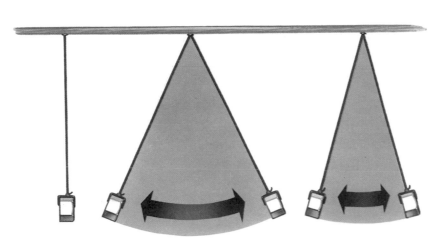

In the Swing

How long is a second? You could say it is 84 centimetres. See why. Tie a heavy iron nut to the end of a length of thread. Hang the thread from a hook so that the thread is 84 centimetres long. Pull the nut to one side and let it swing. You have made a pendulum.

Using your watch, count how many times your pendulum swings in one minute. Back and forth counts as two swings. You will find that your pendulum makes about 60 swings, so each swing takes about a second. Grandfather clocks often have a pendulum with a one-second swing. That is why they are so tall.

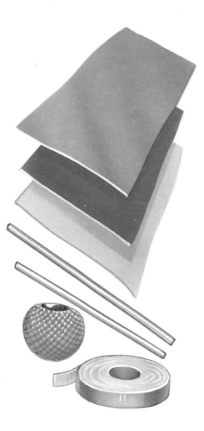

Go Fly a Kite

A kite is a simple flying craft. It works in much the same way as a plane's wing. When it travels at an angle through the air, it rises because of a force pushing up on it, called lift.

Make a Kite

1 You need two wooden sticks about 80 centimetres long, string, tissue or crepe paper, glue or sticky tape.

2 Lash the sticks together at right-angles, with one stick about 15 centimetres from the top of the other.

3 Make nicks in the ends of the sticks and tie string around the outside to make the kite shape.

4 Lay the kite skeleton on the paper and cut around it about two centimetres from the edge.

5 Fold the paper over the string all the way round and stick it in place with glue or tape.

6 Make a tail with folded lengths of paper on a string.

7 Cut a piece of string long enough to tie one end to the top of the kite and the other about two-thirds of the way down. This is the bridle. Notch the stick to keep it in place.

8 Tie a really long string about half-way along the bridle. Then wait for a breezy day and give your kite a test flight.

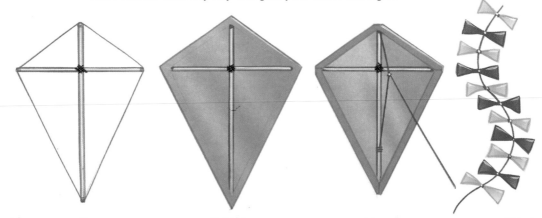

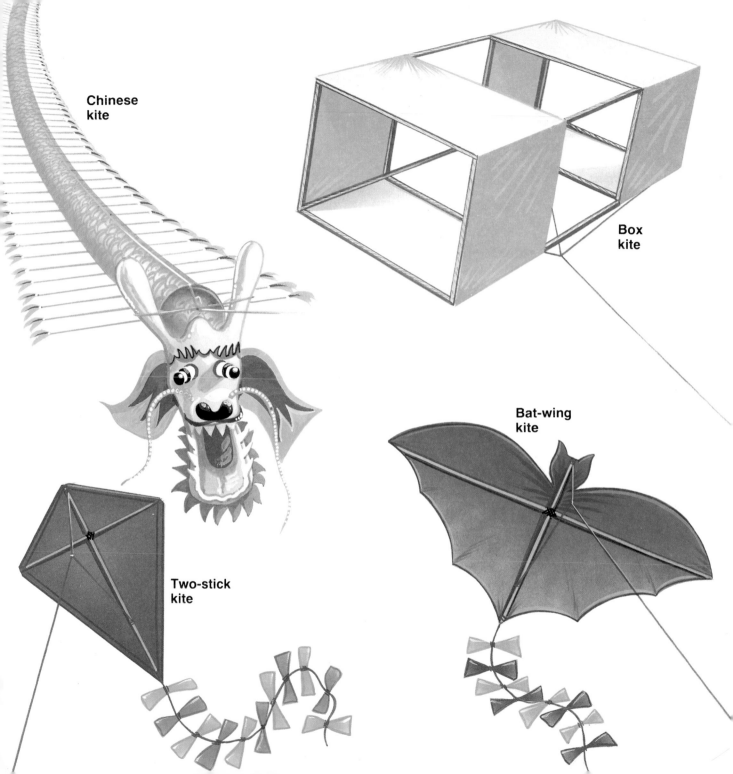

Chinese kite

Box kite

Bat-wing kite

Two-stick kite

Jet Set

Blow up a balloon, pinch the neck and then let it go. See how fast it flies through the air. It is travelling by jet propulsion, just as an aircraft does. The air inside is rushing out in a jet. As the jet of air rushes backwards, the balloon shoots forwards. This effect is called reaction.

Reacting Bottle

1 You need scales, a bottle with a cork, some vinegar and some baking powder.

2 Half fill the bottle with water.

3 Add a little vinegar and a spoonful of baking powder to the bottle and quickly cork it.

4 Place it on the scales and stand back. (The cork will fly out of the bottle.)

5 Watch the scales as the cork shoots out. The bottle will be forced down in the opposite direction – by reaction.

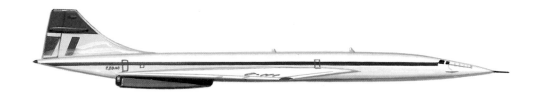

An aircraft jet engine burns fuel to make gases that shoot out backwards. As they shoot backwards, they push the aircraft forwards, by reaction.

Inside the engine, the gases spin turbine wheels before escaping. That is why jets are sometimes called gas-turbine engines. You can make a turbine for yourself.

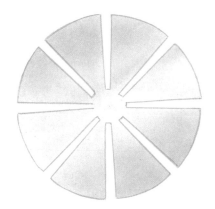

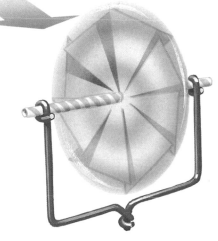

A Turbine Spinner

1 You need a piece of card, a plastic straw and some wire.

2 Cut a disc of card and make a hole in the centre, for the straw to go through.

3 Now cut out little wedges to within half a centimetre of the centre hole.

4 Bend each of the 'blades' of the disc in the same direction.

5 Put the straw through the hole and hang it from a loop of wire fixed to its ends.

6 Blow on the card and see how your turbine spins.

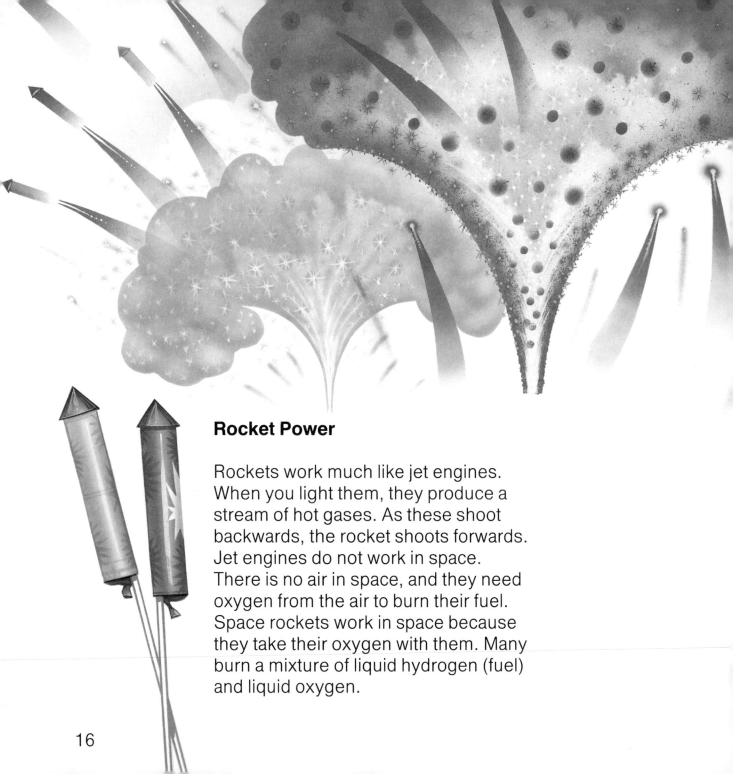

Rocket Power

Rockets work much like jet engines. When you light them, they produce a stream of hot gases. As these shoot backwards, the rocket shoots forwards. Jet engines do not work in space. There is no air in space, and they need oxygen from the air to burn their fuel. Space rockets work in space because they take their oxygen with them. Many burn a mixture of liquid hydrogen (fuel) and liquid oxygen.

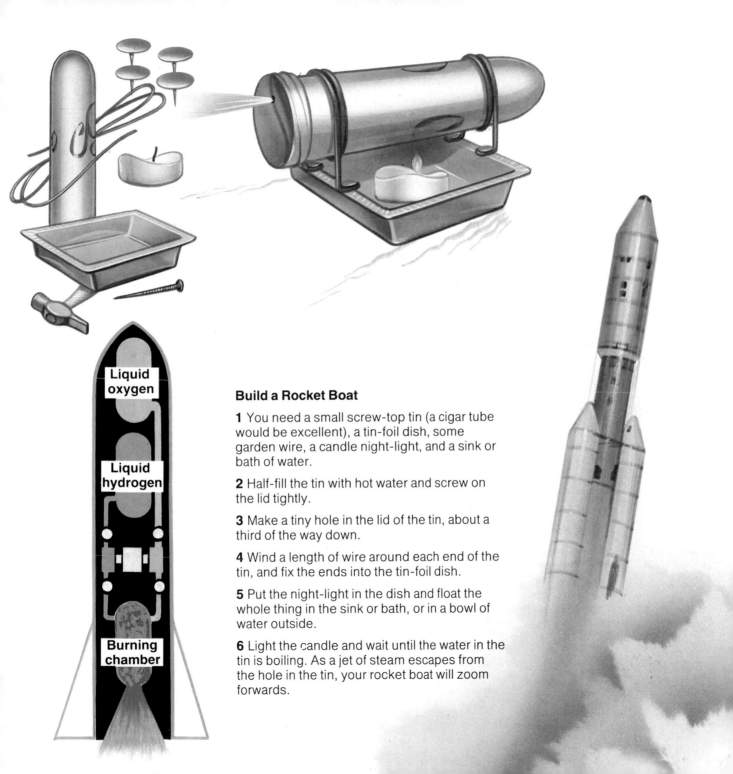

Liquid
oxygen

Liquid
hydrogen

Burning
chamber

Build a Rocket Boat

1 You need a small screw-top tin (a cigar tube would be excellent), a tin-foil dish, some garden wire, a candle night-light, and a sink or bath of water.

2 Half-fill the tin with hot water and screw on the lid tightly.

3 Make a tiny hole in the lid of the tin, about a third of the way down.

4 Wind a length of wire around each end of the tin, and fix the ends into the tin-foil dish.

5 Put the night-light in the dish and float the whole thing in the sink or bath, or in a bowl of water outside.

6 Light the candle and wait until the water in the tin is boiling. As a jet of steam escapes from the hole in the tin, your rocket boat will zoom forwards.

Through a Pinhole

Photography – taking pictures with a camera – is the world's most popular hobby. A camera is basically very simple. It is a box with a hole in one end. The box contains a film which is sensitive to light. When the hole in the box is closed, it is completely dark inside. When it is opened, light rays fall on the film and make a picture. Try making this camera.

An Obscure Camera

1 You need a cardboard tube about 15 centimetres long, some black card, greaseproof paper, black sticky tape, a pin and a sunny day.

2 Cut a disc of card to fit over one end of the tube and make a tiny pinhole in the middle.

3 Tape the disc with black tape to the tube.

4 Tape a piece of greaseproof paper over the other end.

5 On a sunny day, close the curtains so that it is dark inside and poke the pinhole end of the tube into the light.

6 Look at the greaseproof paper and you will see an image of the scene outside. Don't be surprised – it will be the wrong way up, because of the way light travels.

7 The device you have made is called a *camera obscura*. Years ago artists used them for making sketches.

The *camera obscura* focuses a picture on its screen, but you cannot keep a record of what you see. In cameras that contain film you end up with a photograph. Cameras have a shutter over the hole to control how much light enters them, and they have a lens to focus the light. They can take very good pictures. See if you can take a good picture with this shoe-box camera. It works with a pinhole.

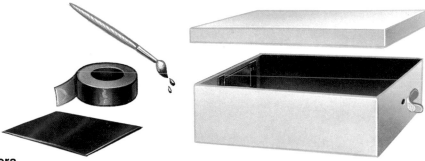

A Pinhole Camera

1 You need a shoe box, a pin, black paint, black tape, sticking plaster, some photographic film (which must not be exposed to light), a dark room and someone to help.

2 Paint the inside of the box and its lid black.

3 Make a pinhole in the centre of one end and tape the sticking plaster over it.

4 Now switch the lights off and make sure the room is absolutely dark. (See that you can lay hands on everything you need before you start. Two people working together will make this easier.)

5 In the dark, tape a piece of photographic film in the centre of the inside wall of the box, directly opposite the pinhole. The dull side should face the pinhole.

6 Still in the dark, put on the lid of the box and tape it round. Your camera is now ready and the

lights can go on again.

7 Place the camera on a table with the pinhole facing the window. Being careful not to move the box, peel off the sticking plaster and leave the camera for about 15 minutes.

8 Restick the plaster. Then, again in the dark, remove the film and put it back in its packet. Take it to a camera shop to be developed and printed.

Sounds Fun

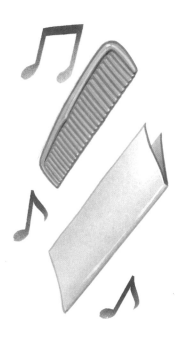

You can have a wail of a time making music with home-made instruments. An old favourite is the comb and paper. The air vibrates between the comb and paper and produces a buzzing sound. But you couldn't call it music!

You can make an even worse noise with a ruler tied to the end of a piece of string. Twirl the ruler in the air (making sure nobody is in the way) and listen to the weird hums, wails and howls that it makes. Pretend there is a storm and your ruler is the wind.

Pan pipes are a set of pipes of different lengths. Each one makes a noise with a different pitch, so that you really can make music. Make them with straws stuck to cardboard. You get sounds of varying pitch, too, if you blow over the necks of bottles part-filled with different amounts of water.

For a really brilliant sound, play the wine glasses. Part-fill wine glasses with different amounts of water. Lightly press a wet finger slowly round and round each rim. The glasses will give out the most beautiful pure notes.

It's For You-hoo

If you want to talk to a friend some distance away without everybody hearing, you can make this simple telephone. You don't have to pay for your calls on it!

Tin Telephone

1 You need two clean cans – the kind that have lids, about 25 metres of twine, a hammer and a nail.

2 Use the hammer and nail to make a hole in the middle of the bottom of each can.

3 Thread the ends of the twine through the holes and tie a large knot inside each tin.

4 Give one can to your friend, and walk away from each other until the string is pulled taut. This is most important.

5 Signal your friend to start talking into his or her can, while you put your can to your ear.

6 You should be able to hear your friend quite well. His voice makes the bottom of his can vibrate. Then the twine carries the vibrations along the bottom of your can and makes that vibrate. Its vibrations set up sound waves, which you hear.

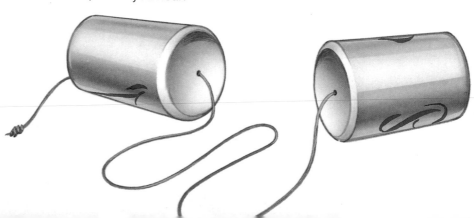

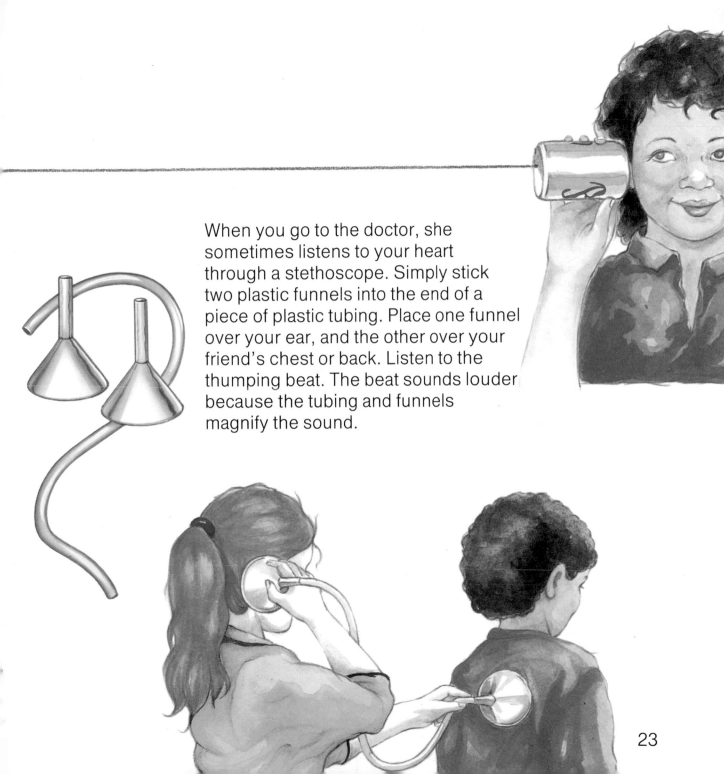

When you go to the doctor, she sometimes listens to your heart through a stethoscope. Simply stick two plastic funnels into the end of a piece of plastic tubing. Place one funnel over your ear, and the other over your friend's chest or back. Listen to the thumping beat. The beat sounds louder because the tubing and funnels magnify the sound.

23

Flashing Messages

You can send a secret coded message to someone with this telegraph set. It uses flashing lights. If you want to send two-way messages you will need two sets between you.

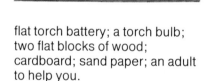

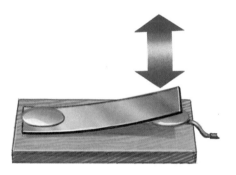

Telegraph Set

1 For each set you need two small strips of tin (You can cut them from an old oil can, but if you do, ask an adult to help you. Thoroughly clean the metal to remove all trace of oil and watch your fingers on the sharp edges.); four drawing pins; three lengths of copper wire (the lengths will depend on how far apart you want your sender and receiver to be, but 15 metres should be more than enough); a

flat torch battery; a torch bulb; two flat blocks of wood; cardboard; sand paper; an adult to help you.

Making the sender

2 Wind a length of copper wire around the shaft of a drawing pin and stick it in one of the blocks of wood (your base board) near the end.

3 Tap a hole for a drawing pin through the end of one of the tin strips.

4 Clean around the hole with sand paper and rub the other end of the strip with sand paper until it is clean and shiny.

5 Wind one end of a length of copper wire around the shaft of the drawing pin, push drawing pin through the hole in the metal strip and into the base board. Position it so the other end of the strip lies over the other drawing pin.

Making the receiver

6 Cut an oblong of cardboard about twice as wide as your metal strip and make a hole in the middle – just big enough for the base of the light bulb.

7 Push the base of the bulb and the third length of copper wire into the hole, so that the wire is touching the metal base of the bulb.

8 Cut out a strip of metal exactly like the one for the sender, with a hole for a drawing pin at each end.

9 Clean the tin strip with sand paper, this time making sure that the middle is shiny clean. Pin it lightly to the second base board.

10 Take the free end of the wire that is attached to the pinned-down end of the sender's metal strip. Wind it around the shaft of one pin, between the strip and the board.

11 Keeping the wire and the strip in position, ease out the pins one at a time and pin the bulb-holder card over the strip. The base of the bulb should touch the strip.

Making Contact

12 Attach the wire from the bulb to one side of the battery.

13 Attach the wire from the drawing pin under the sender strip to the other side of the battery.

14 Now everything is ready. The sender strip is a switch. When it makes contact with the drawing pin underneath, it completes an electrical circuit, and should make the light on the receiver flash on.

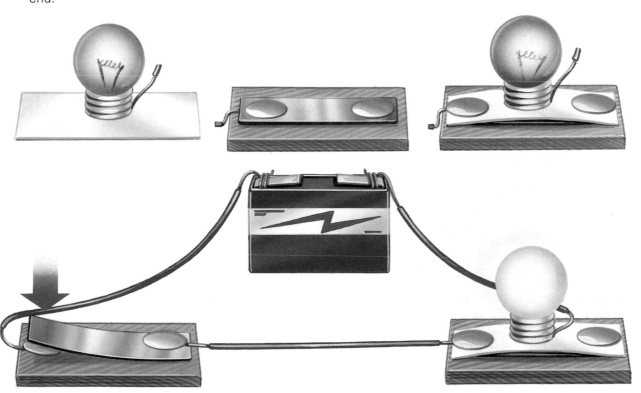

Which Way?

A magnet is a piece of iron or steel that attracts iron and other metals. Buy or borrow two little bar magnets. Hang them up on lengths of string, some way apart from each other. What do you find? They both end up pointing in the same direction — north-south. Magnets always point north because they are being attracted by another big magnet — the Earth itself. It is as if the Earth has a huge magnet buried in it.

You can use a magnet to make a compass.

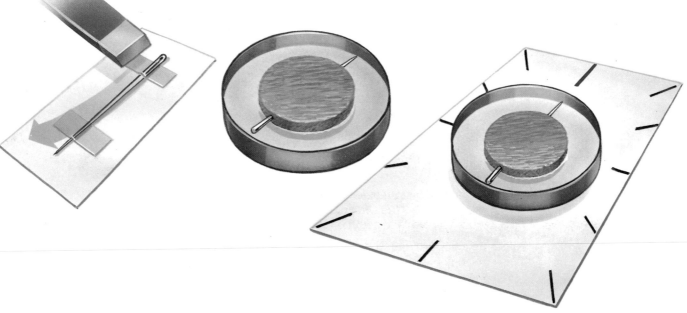

If you haven't got a compass, you can still tell directions – if you have a watch with hands. You point the hour hand at the Sun. Then take a line half way between the hour hand and 12 o'clock. That line points south.

Make a Compass

1 You need a tin lid, a piece of card, a magnet (you can buy them in hobby shops), a cork and a needle.

2 Tape the needle to the card. Then stroke it with one end of the magnet in the same direction about 50 times. Always use the same end of the magnet and lift it at the end of each stroke. By doing this you make the needle into a little magnet. (Test it by picking up a pin with it.)

3 Push the needle through a thin slice of cork and float the cork on water in the tin lid.

4 Draw a compass card, showing the main points of the compass.

5 Place the magnetized needle in its tin on the card. Make sure that the two ends of the needle/magnet are pointing north and south on the card.

6 Check with the Sun that your compass is correct. At midday the Sun lies in the south, and shadows point to the north.

The Main Attraction

If you have ever dropped your pins while you are sewing, you will know how fiddly they are to pick up. If you have a magnet, it is easy to pick up pins. They jump up with no trouble.

If your two bar magnets are not marked, hang them up to see which end points north and which south, and mark them. See what happens when you bring two north ends together, two south ends together, and one south end and one north end together. You can see how magnets attract and repel each other with these experiments.

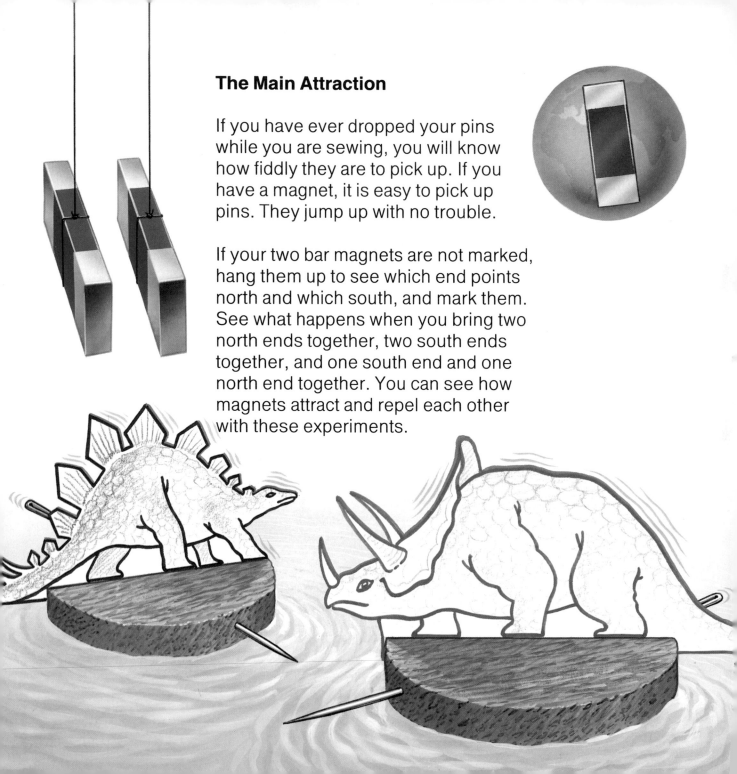

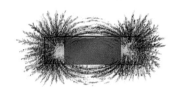

Fun with Filings

1 You need two magnets, card and some iron filings (these are tiny shavings of iron which you can buy with magnets).

2 Sprinkle some iron filings on your magnets. Notice how they cluster round the ends (poles).

3 Place the card over one of the magnets and sprinkle on some filings. Tap the card and notice the pattern that the filings form. This shows the magnetic field of the magnet.

Magnetic Monsters

1 You need two needles, a magnet, two flat corks, some thin card, scissors, colouring pens and a sharp knife.

2 Magnetize the two needles by stroking them with a magnet, as you did on page 26, and stick them through the corks.

3 Draw the most fearsome monsters you can on the card, cut them out and fix them in the cork (in a slit made carefully with the knife).

4 Put your monsters in a bowl of water and watch them jostle each other as the needle magnets push and pull.

Electrifying Activity

Have you heard of an electric lemon? Here is how to make one.

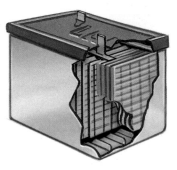

A car battery contains acid.

Electric Lemon

1 You need a soft, juicy lemon, a clean copper nail and a sand-papered strip of zinc from the outer casing of an old dry battery.

2 Stick the nail and the zinc strip into the lemon. Touch them lightly with your tongue. Feel the tingle? Isn't it shocking? What you have done is to make a simple electric cell, or battery. It works by the chemical action of the copper and zinc with the acid (juice) in the lemon.

See how electricity and magnetism go together. Set up the telegraph circuit you made on pages 24 and 25. Next to one of the wires, place the compass you made on page 26. Press the switch and see how the needle moves. This shows that a wire carrying an electric current becomes magnetic.

You can increase this magnetism by winding the wire round an iron bolt.

Make an Electromagnet

1 You need your switch, your battery, a long length of wire, an iron bolt, and some pins and other metal things to pick up.

2 Wind the wire round the bolt and attach it to your battery and switch.

3 Hold the bolt near some pins or paper clips and switch on. The bolt has become a magnet and attracts the pins.

4 Switch off, and the pins fall away. The bolt has lost its magnetism. It is a temporary magnet, or electromagnet.

Index and glossary